caution

Eating marijuana can be a very potent form of consumption. Please read all the dosage information and cautions about consuming marijuana in this fashion, before you make any of the recipes in this book.

This book is for informational purposes only. The author has endeavored to present as accurate information as is possible on this subject, in which research has been limited, due to the fact that Cannabis remains illegal.

The author does not advocate breaking any laws, and cannot be held responsible for how the information in this book is used.

Design — Studio Graphik, SF
Edited by Dana Cannazopoulous
Photography by Tom Flowers

. . . with love to PJ, Jenny X, DMZ and π

marijuana herbal cookbook

by

Tom Flowers

ISBN# 0-9647946-0-8
ISBN 13# 978-0-9647946-0-3

First Printing September 1995
Second Printing February 1996
Third Printing December 1997
Fourth Printing October 2002

table of contents

preface

When I first started researching this book I was well aware of how high you could get eating marijuana. Practically every pothead has a tale of being dosed on a marijuana confection.

Sometimes this occurs because of the lack of information on the subject of marijuana and cooking. People who don't have accurate recipes tend to make their baked goods too strong. Also, many times people seem to have a "yahoo" approach to eating pot. And since the high doesn't come on for about an hour, there's ample time to eat more or too much. Other times I have seen people totally disregard the cook's instructions, "because, well, like, it's only pot".

Many cooks I know purposely make low dosage foods simply to compensate for this.

Other than to tell people, "WARNING, if you eat another cookie you will soon be approaching warp speed", there is little this author can do to prevent overuse, other than to offer accurate information. I also think I have given good reasons to be careful, and to have respect for marijuana eaten in food and capsules. If the book sometimes reads like a "flashing yellow light", it is because it seems warranted.

Information on dosage and preparing marijuana to cook with, are as important as the recipes them selves. After all, once you know how to get the marijuana ready, and how much you will use per dose, you can cook marijuana into practically anything.

I have endeavored to give you, the reader, as accurate a view as possible as to how people are using marijuana in cooking. Many thanks to the cooks in the San Francisco Bay Area who have granted me access to their information and kitchens. Many of them are "new age" herbalists using marijuana for medicine rather than fun.

As one shaman cook told me "marijuana may not be the cure, but it makes looking for it interesting".

Tom Flowers
Oakland, 1995

Why Cook?

There are many reasons to cook with marijuana, including concerns about the safety of smoking, and the different effects marijuana seems to have when eaten rather than when smoked. Marijuana, when cooked into food in high doses, can act like a long lasting, organic psychedelic drug. You can get very high eating marijuana.

Another reason marijuana cooking is becoming popular is the renewed interest in marijuana as medicine. Before it was outlawed in 1937, cannabis extracts made with an alcohol base, to be taken by the teaspoon, were common. Marijuana, when taken orally, has many medicinal qualities. Certain medical effects, such as pain relief or anti-inflammation, are more pronounced when the marijuana is eaten.

Cooking is a somewhat neglected art as far as the cannabis plant is concerned. Smoking, at least up to now, has been the preferred method used to consume the drug, for both pleasure and medicinal use.

This preference has been changing for a number of reasons. One of the main ones is the availability of marijuana leaf. This is a by-product of domestic sinsemilla production. It does not make a good smoke, since it is so harsh and comparatively low in THC, the chemical in marijuana that gets you high. Commercial growers treat it as waste, because they have problems selling it. When used in cooking, marijuana leaf, rather than being a harsh smoke or waste product, is a potent, good-tasting herb.

Another reason some people cook with marijuana is the ease with which marijuana consumption can be kept secret. Without its distinct odor, very noticeable when smoked, marijuana can be hard to detect. A capsule, a cookie, a piece of cake, or even an entrée, can disguise cannabis easily. Few people will know that you will be getting very high from that

Certain medical effects, such as pain relief or anti-inflammation, are more pronounced when the marijuana is eaten.

innocent-looking brownie. You can eat marijuana in places where you would never smoke a joint.

Many people who use pot medicinally smoke 5 or 6 joints each day. This can become a real problem, especially if the person is trying to keep a job. Eating pot allows the person to take the drug less often and in ways not likely to be noticed by other workers.

The Differences Between Eating and Smoking

There are some distinct differences both in the onset and in the duration of the high when marijuana is eaten. When pot is smoked, the high comes on quickly, usually within ten minutes. It may take an hour or longer for the high to come on when marijuana is eaten.

When smoked, the high may last up to 3 hours, while when eaten, the high can last 5 hours or more. Some of the medicinal effects can last up to 12 hours when the pot is eaten.

The qualities of the high can also be quite distinct between the two methods of ingesting pot. Many people compare the effects of eating pot to "tripping", although this seems to be dose related. It is possible to eat pot and not get high at all, but still get medicinal effects, which are present even in small doses. For example, only small doses are needed to stimulate the appetite. Controlling the dose is the key to controlling how high a consumer will get.

Though it is unlikely that a person will overdose while smoking marijuana, it is possible to overdose when eating. The high comes on slowly when pot is ingested, and it may take over an hour to feel the full effects. Caution must be taken both by the cook and the eater. Foods must be prepared in such a way that not too much pot is ingested before the effects are felt. The person eating the pot must remain aware of how much has been consumed.

I really must emphasize the importance of regulating the

dosage of marijuana to both the cook and the consumer. Respect this drug as you would any other psychedelic drug. It sometimes hard to get this point across because people think we are just talking about getting high on pot. But this is pot in a different and, depending on dosage, more potent form. One half to one gram of marijuana leaf is very easy to bake into a cookie and will get most people quite high. More than that might induce auditory and visual alterations which some people will consider pleasant. These alterations increase with dosage. As with other organic psychedelic drugs, such as peyote and psilocybin mushrooms, some people may be uncomfortable with these effects. Consuming more than 4 grams of good quality leaf is likely to make many people sick rather than high. I urge you to use all due caution when using higher dosages.

As the cook, if you decide to make a very potent dessert, make sure your guests know what they are getting, and that they don't get too much of it. See the dosage section for specific information.

Why Marijuana Gets You High

Tetrahydrocannabinol, or delta 9 THC, is the most potent drug agent contained in marijuana. THC, which comes in many forms called isomers, is a sub-group of the cannabinoids, monoterpene compounds, of which 50 have been isolated (Ott, *Parmacotheon* 1993). It is the interaction of the different cannabinoids that give varieties of marijuana their particular highs, and also their distinct scent. Some grass may be "speedy", some "sleepy", some might be thought-provoking, or enhance your mood.

Mood enhancement may be one of the marijuana high's most prominent features. It helps explain why the same marijuana seems to have different effects when taken at different times. If someone is tired, the grass may put them to sleep. If they need to clarify an event in their life, they may stay up and speed-rap with a friend. Or they may become contemplative, and the high might turn into a meditative trance.

Capitate glands
and sharp cystolith
hairs on leaf, 40x;
Inset: Capitate glands
on flower, 50x

The psychoactive cannabinoids, including THC, are all contained in the capitate glands. These glands cover most leaves, but occur in the highest density on the flowers of marijuana. The only leaves with little potency are the fan leaves, the large leaves on the main stem around which branches form.

The number of glands found on the pot do not always indicate its potency - ultimately it's what's in the glands that counts. However, a count of the glands should give some idea of how potent the pot is. It is easy to inspect drug glands on marijuana with a magnifying glass.

One distinction between marijuana and most other drugs is that the cannabinoids are contained in an oil base. Most other drugs are alkaloids and are water-based. In cooking this distinction is quite important, since the cook wants to produce a product through which the marijuana is evenly distributed, and which will take effect as quickly as possible. To do this the outer layer of the capitate glands must be dissolved, and the oils they contain evenly distributed throughout the food.

Both oils and alcohol do a fine job of breaking down and dissolving the capitate glands. Once dissolved, the oils in the glands can be evenly mixed into the chosen recipe.

When mixed with oil, the natural emulsifier lecithin is helpful in dissolving the capitate glands and making the pot ready for cooking.

Water, even hot water, does a poor job of dissolving the drug glands. Many of the glands will remain intact in water. If pot is drunk for example, in a tea that has no milk in it, the pot will be slowly absorbed, and the effects will be unpredictable.

The recipes in this book will tell you the best ways to ingest the cannabinoids with your food. Getting the maximum effect from the amount of herb used is easy when cooking.

Haphazardly concocted foods can make for an unpredictable high, or no high at all. With an understanding of how the drug works, anyone can turn out foods appreciated by all.

Hemp Seed and Oil

Hemp seed contains 20% complete protein and about 30% oil. The sterile seed is legal to possess in the U.S., except in Kentucky and Florida. Hemp seeds are not psychoactive. A few pamphlets on cooking with hemp seed are available. Because of the novelty of using cannabis that is actually legal, I will include a few recipes here.

That said, I have some reservations on using both the seed and the oil as they are presently available. Hemp seed must be imported into the U.S. because it is not legal to grow even non-drug varieties of cannabis. The seed remains legal because of a concession made to bird keepers when pot was outlawed in 1937. It is brought into the country as bird food. By law the seed must also be sterilized, usually by steaming, so the seeds cannot be grown.

Once hemp seed is cooked it has a short shelf life; it should be refrigerated and used quickly. Oil made from the seed should be pressed soon after the seed is sterilized and refrigerated. Most of the hemp seed and oil I have seen has not been refrigerated. As of this writing small amounts of oil pressed from live seed is being shipped into the country frozen. If you are looking for a source of uncooked seeds you might try seeded marijuana. Seeds from marijuana, like hemp, are not psychoactive and are similar in flavor.

Because of the real potential of rancidity, I suggest that you don't eat large amounts of hemp seed meal or oil. In small amounts the meal is palatable, and adds its own flavor to foods. If you decide to add hemp seed oil to your diet use it in recipes that do not call for long cooking. In small amounts it's good in salad dressings. It can also be drizzled over cooked veggies or used generally as a butter substitute. Long cooking will destroy many of the healthy facets of hemp oil.

Hemp oil has strong medicinal quantities stemming from its high content of Omega 3, Omega 6 and Omega 9 fatty acids. These components of hemp oil are known to be helpful in lowering cholesterol and lessening inflammatory conditions due to auto-immune diseases like rheumatoid arthritis. The usual dosage is one tablespoonful or more per day. The oil can also be used in preparing marijuana capsules. (See page 73.)

Cooking with ground hemp seed is easy. The hull and the meal of the seed are difficult to separate, but the whole seed can be lightly roasted and ground into a flour-like meal for use in cooking. This can be done in a coffee mill, a food processor, or even a good blender.

When using hemp seed, remember that it contains 30% oil, more than high grade ice cream. Since it is so rich, small amounts of hemp seed meal are used in most recipes. In general, hemp seed meal can be substituted for about 10% of the wheat flour or other starch called for in a recipe. Always refrigerate leftovers and consume quickly.

Using the Plant

Psychoactive cooking with cannabis is relatively inexpensive if leaf is used. Since leaf has little monetary value, growers often give it away or sell it for very little. These growers aren't necessarily showing great magnanimity, they really like getting rid of leaf. It has little economic value but is just as illegal as the flowers.

This fact points out the only downside of using leaf.

Marijuana activists fundraising and registering voters for the 1980 California ballot initiative to legalize marijuana for personal use.

In the eyes of the law a $300 pound of leaf is equal to a pound of manicured sinsemilla, which may cost $4,000. Trust the government not to know the difference between flowers and shake.

Though it makes a harsh smoke and for this reason is shunned, leaf actually contains sizable amounts of psychoactive ingredients. It often contains 1/8 or more of the THC found in the flowers. The leaf trimmed from sinsemilla flowers when they are manicured is especially potent. The flowers themselves may also be used in cooking, though they are far more expensive.

You might have to smoke 3 joints or more of leaf to match the high of a joint of high quality sinsemilla. Cooking and eating the same amount of leaf is easy, tastes good and gets you higher, although the effect takes longer to come on. One cookie or other confection can easily contain all the pot that is needed.

All kinds of pot, including sinsemilla or imports like Thai, Mexican or hashish, can be used for cooking. Because of the differing potency of many kinds of marijuana, dosage considerations will play an important part in cooking with the different kinds of cannabis.

Dosage Considerations

The kind of pot used in cooking and how high you want to get are important considerations. One may want only a medical dose, that has medicinal effect but does not get a person very high. Or one may want to go on a "trip". Either way dosage is very important, because it is possible to overdose eating marijuana.

The effects of an overdose are not usually alarming, but can include dizziness and passing out. Most overdosed people fall asleep relatively quickly, and all that is necessary is to keep them calm until they do. But there is no reason for overdosing and the cook must take responsibility. Even experienced marijuana smokers should be cautious when eating marijuana.

Dosage considerations are based not only on the amount of THC in the pot, but the body size and experience of the person using it. Go lower on dosage for smaller people and novices. On the low end we are talking about as little as 1/2 gram of leaf or only 1/8 gram of sinsemilla flowers.

That said, we can give some generalities about the potencies of different kinds of marijuana, though the cook will have to make final determination about a plant's potency. A toke or two could be helpful.

High grade domestic flowers contain an average of 4-7% THC. Most imported marijuana averages 2-4% THC. Exotic varieties, like Thai, are variable, sometimes as potent as Sinsemilla, but usually containing 3-5% THC. Hashish has the largest range and can contain 2-10% THC. Most hash contains 5-7% THC. Leaf from sinsemilla, containing bud trim, is about 1-2% THC.

For a person who weighs 150 pounds, who has some experience using marijuana, and who wants to get high, a single dose ranges from:

- Marijuana leaf: 1/2 to 2 grams
- Imported marijuana flowers: 1/4 to 1 gram (less seeds)
- Hashish: 1/8 to 2 grams (since hash varies so much in potency, smoking some before using it in cooking will help gauge its strength)
- Sinsemilla flowers: 1/8 to 1/2 gram

Regular users may not get very high from the lowest dose. However, people who weigh significantly less than 150 pounds could get quite high on one half gram of leaf. The lowest dose will also have medicinal effects; for example, appetite stimulation.

Recipes in this book are given in both the higher and lower range. Please use lower doses until you are accustomed to eating pot. You can always eat another cookie, or consume more cake, *after* you feel the effects.

It is easy enough to fit the total dosage in a *single cookie* or brownie, so use caution.

Keep in mind that the dosages cited are the totals that should be consumed for 4-5 hours. It is easy enough to fit the total dosage in a single cookie or brownie, so use caution.

Treating Overdose

When smoked there seems to be a marijuana plateau. You get just so high, then, unless you smoke several joints in succession, you don't really get beyond this plateau. When pot is eaten there seems to be no such constraints.

In high doses it is possible to have a full-fledged psychedelic experience. Such an experience would be enjoyed by many, and tolerated by most others. For the few who inadvertently find themselves in such a situation, and don't like it, there are a few things that can be done.

The most important thing is for the person to realize that they are in no physical danger. Though they may experiencing a distorted reality, it would take enormous doses of marijuana to do any permanent physical harm.

The person should sit or lie down and try to relax, as dizziness may be one of the symptoms. Chills may be another symptom that is easy to treat, by keeping the person warm.

Though the person will be high for 4 or 5 hours, the most intense feelings will occur within an hour after the effects begin coming on. Keep the person calm until then, and continue to reassure them throughout the "peak" of the high.

Avoiding overdose is one of the best reasons to monitor the amount of loaded food a person consumes, especially a guest. Needless to say, never give people spiked food without their knowledge.

The thoughts of an experienced marijuana eater may help illustrate what can be expected: "In my experience, the peak of a 1/2 to 1 gram (leaf) cookie happens about 1 hour and 20 minutes after eating. The peak of a 2 gram cookie happens almost 2 hours after eating. I start feeling the effects about 55 minutes after eating, unless I had a very empty stomach to start with - then onset happens within 30 minutes. Once I have hit the peak, which is like smoking, but more intense, I stay there for 2 or 3 hours. I then slowly come down, being back to 'normal' in about 6 or 7 hours. If I eat after about 9pm, I will still feel some effects (lassitude, low energy) the next morning -nothing a large cup of coffee won't cure. A friend who has been eating 1 to 1.5 grams per day for several months agrees with my estimate of onset and peaking times, though the effects do not last as long for him."

It should also be mentioned that people eating marijuana should refrain using other drugs, like alcohol. The marijuana itself will be quite potent enough, and the other drugs might even detract from the experience.

Preparing Pot for Use

There are many options for getting marijuana ready for use in cooking. The easiest one is to turn the pot into a flour.

Leaf Flour

To make a flour from marijuana leaf the pot is first cleaned of any twigs or other woody debris. It should be dry and break apart when crushed. If it isn't dry put it in a slow 200° F oven for 15 minutes or a microwave for a minute or two.

The pot is then put through a food processor or other grinding device, like a flour mill. Food processors get the marijuana down to a fine particulate stage. For best results in cooking the marijuana should be ground up further in a coffee grinder, which reduces it to a fine powder. After this, put the

powder through a flour sifter or screen to remove any remaining debris. Store the flour in the refrigerator or freezer.

When processing marijuana, a white dust may be kicked up, especially if the pot is very dry. Rather than dust, this is actually the capitate glands, the potent part of marijuana. Be careful when handling - let the dust settle before opening the grinder or processor, and collect any dust that may escape.

Flower Flour

To process buds into flour, the flowers must be very dry. Make the flowers crisp by putting them in a microwave for a couple of minutes, or for 10 minutes in an oven 300° F. Once the flowers cool they should be crisp. The flowers are then removed carefully from their stalks and ground. A coffee grinder works well, and can easily process moderate amounts of cannabis flowers.

Another method of preparing bud is to separate the flowers from any woody material and put them in a blender. Then add the liquid from a recipe, preferably with some alcohol or oil in it, and puree together. Alcohol and oil help dissolve the glands which hold the THC.

Substituting Flowers or Hash for Leaf Flour

Note: 1 ounce = 28 grams

Marijuana Leaf Flour	.5 ounce	.8 ounce	1 ounce	2 ounce
	14 grams	22.4 grams		
Regular Mexican, Jamaican, or Columbian	7 grams	11 grams	14 grams	1 ounce
High Grade Imports or good Thai	3 grams	5 grams	6 grams	12 grams
Good Domestic Sinsemilla good hash, great Thai	1.75 grams	3 grams	3.5 grams	7 grams
Excellent Sinsemilla great hash	1.25 grams	2 grams	2.5 grams	5 grams

Using Hashish

Owing to the fact that hash is usually made with some oil, it is ready to use once it is dissolved. Hashish can be dissolved in a little hot water, or with a little warm oil, milk, or melted butter.

Hash is often mixed in coffee or chocolate drinks. A single dose of good hash ranges from 1/8 to 1/2 gram. Be careful with hash however, because its potency varies widely.

Substituting Marijuana Flowers or Hashish in the Recipes of This Book

Many of the recipes in this book call for using marijuana leaf flour. They can easily be adapted to use marijuana flowers or hashish. The most important variable is the potency of the stash. If the recipe calls for the indicated amounts of leaf flour, substitute marijuana flowers (less seed) as shown in the chart.

The only other thing the cook has to do is add a small amount of wheat flour, to substitute for the marijuana leaf flour. An ounce of marijuana leaf flour is about 1/3 cup. If you were to use regular Mexican marijuana in a recipe you would use about half as much as leaf (about 1/6 cup). So you would also add about 1/6 cup of wheat flour to the recipe. Another example, if you want to use excellent sinsemilla in place of an ounce of marijuana leaf (1/3 cup), you would add almost 1/3 cup of wheat flour to the recipe also, because only about a tablespoon of powdered flowers will be used.

Extracts and Concentrates

As people get more into cannabis cooking, they may come to appreciate extracts. They might see the wisdom of having a few pounds of butter, or a liter of oil or rum, rather than a pound of marijuana sitting around. Some cooks will also like the fact that recipes made with marijuana butter, oil, or alcohol extract don't have the characteristic green color that foods made with marijuana leaf have.

The capitate glands containing the psychoactive cannabinoids in marijuana can be dissolved with either alcohol or oil. This is the basis of extracts. The glands open, and the THC dissolves in a base of oil or alcohol. Processing pot in this way aids in the absorption of the drug, when it is eaten.

Using extracts opens up a whole new realm of cooking, as extracts and concentrates can be added to all kinds of foods and drinks. They can even be used in making beer or wine. Extracts using alcohol can also be concentrated, and taken by the teaspoon.

As was mentioned when you use extracts or concentrates in cooking, you won't get the green color in food, so prominent when leaf is used. The food you make containing extracts will look just like regular food. Many cooks will find this appealing both for aesthetic reasons and for secrecy.

The capitate glands containing the psychoactive cannabinoids in marijuana can be dissolved with either alcohol or oil.

On the other hand, you might like the green color marijuana leaf imparts, because it clearly delineates the fact that this is not regular food. There is less chance that it will be eaten by mistake.

Extracts are not difficult to make. Though they do take some time, they can be made in quantity and stored in the refrigerator or freezer.

Alcohol Extracts

Extracts, using liquor as the solvent to dissolve the THC glands, are easy to make. It only takes a few days of soaking before most of the drug glands have dissolved. Any liquor can be used for this process. The higher the proof (percentage of alcohol), the faster the process. Some rum for example is 151 proof or 75% pure alcohol. Though expensive, the high proof liquors do the best job of dissolving the capitate glands, which hold the cannabinoids. Though the extract may be high in alcohol in the beginning most of it can be evaporated off as the extract is concentrated. Little or no alcohol need remain in the final product.

"Mari-Rum" is a favorite among people who make extracts. But what kind of extract is made really depends on what you like. Marijuana extracts have been made with vodka and gin, which have a neutral taste, or even whiskey. (See Firewater, page 35). Sweet liqueurs such as Kahlua can be added as a flavoring to the above, or can be used by themselves. Liqueurs contain less alcohol and so the mixture must steep for a longer time.

If you do decide to drink marijuana liquor, be forewarned. The alcohol should be used only as a carrier for the marijuana. Large amounts of pot and alcohol will make you sick. This truly is the drink to have, when you are only drinking one.

Another option for liquor extracts is to concentrate the extract for use in cooking. This is done by letting the liquor sit in the open air, where it evaporates relatively quickly. As the alcohol dissipates it helps to evaporate any water that is in the liquor. If you expose 4 cups of liquor to air, in a pan wide enough so that the liquor is about one inch deep, 2 cups should evaporate in about 12 hours.

Some sources suggest using heat to speed up making a concentrate, but this is not necessary, and it can be dangerous. It is easy to see how exposing alcohol to an open flame can cause a fire. However, heating alcohol to high temperatures even on an electric stove can be hazardous. This is because alcohol rapidly releases fumes when heated. The fumes are volatile and can easily catch fire.

If you want to speed up the extraction process, expose the alcohol to more air (use a bigger pan), and the alcohol will evaporate faster. An 80 proof liquor (40 percent alcohol) can be safely heated once the alcohol concentration is less than 20 percent. In practical terms, this means when more than half of the liquid has evaporated. If you use 151 proof rum, when 1/4 of the liquid remains the alcohol concentration should be below 20 percent. With that in mind, here is a recipe for making a concentrate from marijuana leaf.

Marijuana Leaf Concentrate

1. Wash 4 ounces of whole marijuana leaf in tepid, 90°F, water. (It is best to use whole leaf, because once wet and pliable, you can wring it dry by hand, like a sponge.) When you swish the leaf around in the water, a lot of the chlorophyll will be removed. Dump the water and pot through a sieve or colander. Lightly wring out the excess water from the pot. You can skip this step if you don't mind a very green concentrate.

2. Put the pot in a bowl and cover with 4 cups of 80 proof liquor, such as rum, vodka, gin or whiskey. Stir the mixture to a uniform consistency making sure the marijuana leaf is covered. Cover the mix-

ture and let it sit 2 days or more.

3. Next, take the cover off the mix and let it sit open to the air overnight.

4. When about half the liquid remains stir the mixture again, and then pour it through a fine sieve or coffee filter, making sure to catch the liquid. Press the leaf to push out any remaining liquid, and then thoroughly wring any remaining liquid out of the leaf by hand.

5. Pour 1/2 cup of the liquid you collect back through the leaf, and repeat the steps above. You should have about two cups of concentrate.

These 2 cups of concentrate can be boiled down further on low heat, or it can be used as is. One teaspoon is a moderate dose.

The extract recipes in this book call for simmering these 2 cups down to 1 cup. At this point the extract will contain little alcohol but will be quite potent. It will have a potency of about 60 - 70% of the 4 ounces of the marijuana leaf it was made from. This is equal to about 70-80 1 gram doses of leaf. About 1/2 teaspoon will equal a one gram dose, so be very careful when adding this concentrate to recipes.

This extract can easily be added to any recipe you choose in place of another liquid ingredient. If a recipe calls for water, wine, milk or some other liquid, for example, the marijuana concentrate can easily be substituted.

If you want to try to make use of the THC remaining in the leaf left over from making extract, you can make a tea.

Extract Tea

Boil the leaf left over from making the extract in 6 cups of water. Steep for 15 minutes, to remove any remaining alcohol. The tea has a strong peppery herb flavor. Dilute with up to 6 more cups water, until it is palatable. This tea will have some sweetness from the liqueur used in the extract and you can add more if you like. Add lemon, herbs or other teas to taste. Also, it's good iced.

The tea as described has low psychoactive properties. You might need 2 or 3 cups to get high. The tea is good for relaxing the stomach, and has been used to stimulate the appetite. It is also reported to be helpful in treating cramps and indigestion.

Butter Extracts

Butter extracts are the favored way to concentrate THC for cooking. Butter does a fine job extracting

THC. You can extract more THC with butter than with alcohol extracts using 80 proof liquor. Butter extracts are about 80% as potent as the marijuana they are made from. Butter extracts are also inexpensive and easy to make. They don't require high grade pot, but they do take some time.

Because butter can be used so easily in cooking, marijuana butter can easily be integrated into countless recipes of your choice.

To make a butter extract with leaf use the following recipe. (To make butter with Marijuana flowers see page 14 for substitutions.)

1. Heat: 5 cups of water
   Add: 4 ounces of marijuana leaf
   1 pound butter (2 cups)
   note: For each additional ounce of leaf, add 1/4 pound of butter (1/2 cup), and 1 cup of water.

A potato ricer is used to press the butter and water from the leaf. Right: The finished product— marijuana butter.

2. Bring to a boil, then cover and simmer on low heat for 1 1/2 -2 hours. Stir occasionally.
3. Strain the mix, retaining the liquid. A baby food sieve or potato ricer is helpful in pressing out the butter and water that remains in the leaf.
4. Boil 2 cups of water, and pour over the leaf to remove any leftover butter. Press again.
5. Let the mixture set until the butter and water separate. The liquid is then put in the refrigerator or for faster processing, in the freezer.
6. When cooled, the butter and pot will congeal on

top of the water. Collect the hardened butter extract and refrigerate. Discard the water.

Note: You will get a little less butter back than you put in as about 1/4 cup will remain in the leaf. Because of this 1/2 cup of marijuana butter will have virtually the same potency as one ounce of marijuana leaf. Use it cautiously.

Adding butter extracts to food is simple. You could spread a little on an english muffin or toast, for example, or melt some on vegetables. Keep in mind however, a moderate dose of marijuana butter is less than 1 teaspoon, for a 160 pound, (73 kg), person. Marijuana butter can be made at lower strengths by adding more butter or less pot.

Vegetable Oil Extracts

Oil extracts can be made in the same fashion as the marijuana butter extract above. Just substitute 2 cups of oil for the pound of butter in that recipe.

That said, some special handling is needed to make marijuana oil. Basically, you use the freezer instead of the refrigerator. Here is an easy method of making marijuana oil. Simmer the oil, pot, and water as in the marijuana butter recipe. Strain and cool. Let the oil and water thoroughly separate, then put the mix in the freezer. The water will freeze, and the oil can be poured off.

Most people let the mix set in the freezer overnight, but the ice should be solid in four to six hours depending on the freezer. Wait until the ice is solid to remove the oil, for best results.

Some vegetable oils like olive and peanut oils will harden when frozen. They can be easily scraped off the surface of the ice, with a spoon or spatula. Always refrigerate marijuana oil. It will keep for more than a month. For longer term storage it can be frozen.

Use marijuana oil in the same proportions and in the same way as you would use marijuana butter. A moderate dose of marijuana oil is less than 1 teaspoon. Be cautious with its use.

Substituting Marijuana Butter or Oil for Marijuana Leaf Flour

Most of the recipes in this book are written to be made with marijuana leaf flour. This is because it takes time to concoct an extract. It's the old "I want to get high now, damn it" syndrome.

Since butter is used in many of the recipes in this book, marijuana butter is easily integrated into these recipes. One - half cup of marijuana butter (1/4 pound) equals approximately 1 ounce (28 grams) of marijuana leaf flour.

If you want to substitute marijuana butter for leaf, just take out the leaf and add marijuana butter in the right amount. If a recipe calls for 1/2 ounce of marijuana leaf, for example, you would add 1/8 pound (1/4 cup) of marijuana butter. You would also omit 1/4 cup of regular butter from the recipe.

Wheat flour should also be added to recipes as a substitute for the marijuana leaf flour that is being taken out. For example, if you add 1/2 cup of marijuana butter to a recipe, this equals 1 ounce of marijuana leaf flour, which is about 1/3 cup. So you add 1/3 cup of wheat flour to the recipe. This is to keep the recipe at the right consistency.

Let's look at the recipe for the cookie Greenies to illustrate:

GREENIES

oven to 300° F

Mix together
   3/4 cup melted butter or oil
   3/4 cup milk, soy milk or half & half

7 teaspoons-2/3 cup (.5-2 ounces)
marijuana leaf flour

1 egg

Beat for 5 minutes.

Mix in

3/4 cup sugar

1 teaspoon orange extract (optional)

1/2 teaspoon nutmeg (optional)

Sift in

1 teaspoon baking powder

2 cups flour

Beat with a mixer until thoroughly blended. Spoon onto a greased cooking sheet by the tablespoon. Bake 25-30 minutes.

Yield: 28 small cookies

Let's say you wanted use marijuana butter or oil to make these cookies, and you wanted each cookie to have the potency of 1 gram of marijuana leaf flour. To modify the recipe you would: Add 1/2 cup marijuana butter or oil, and 1/3 cup of wheat flour. You would omit marijuana leaf flower and 1/2 cup of the regular butter called for.

All the recipes in which marijuana butter or oil can be used in place of marijuana leaf flour are marked in the recipe section.

Do not exceed the recommended dosage. For example, if the recipe calls for one ounce of marijuana leaf flour do not add more than 1/2 cup of marijuana butter or oil. If the recipe calls for 1/2 ounce (14 grams) of marijuana leaf flour, use no more than 1/4 cup (4 tablespoons) of marijuana butter or oil.

Lecithin, Milk and Soy

Lecithin is a natural product, high in certain B vitamins, found in both cow and soy milk. It is an emulsifier, preventing oils from separating from other liquids. When you shake up a liquid containing lecithin, oil, and other liquids, like water or vinegar, the oil will be dispersed in small droplets, throughout the solution. Though lecithin will not dissolve the drug

In India, preparations combining marijuana and milk have been used for centuries.

glands on marijuana, like oil or alcohol, it is very helpful in processing marijuana for use in cooking. For example, due to the lecithin in milk, even milk that is only 2% fat will dissolve the drug glands on pot. This is because, even though there is only a small amount of fat in the milk, it is evenly distributed, and will surround and dissolve the THC glands, especially when heated.

In India, preparations combining marijuana and milk have been used for centuries. Bhang, for example, is a concoction using pot and milk which can be cooked down and added to food, or used immediately to make milk drinks like Bhang Lassi. (See page 33.)

Soy milk also contains lecithin, and enough oil to make marijuana ready to imbibe.

Marijuana milk can be made for a single serving, or as a kind of concentrate. For four single servings:
1. Bring to a boil 1 quart of cow or soy milk.
2. Stir in 2-4 teaspoons of marijuana leaf flour
3. Sweeten to taste
4. Simmer (don't boil) for 30 minutes
5. Strain and Drink

Note : This mix will increase in potency if it is simmered longer or if it is left to cool before it is strained. It will also be more potent if the leaf is not strained out.

When making a milk concentrate, the potency will be determined by the amount of marijuana used. If you simmer an ounce (28 grams) of marijuana leaf in a quart of milk, you will get about 30 moderate doses. This is about 1 fluid ounce of milk per dose. Fresh milk will keep for about a week under refrigeration. It can be frozen for longer storage.

Lecithin can also be added to any recipe when it is helpful to keep the ingredients mixed, such as salad dressings or soups where the oil tends to separate

24

and float to the top. Very little lecithin is needed; only 1/2 teaspoon of lecithin powder per recipe will do the trick.

Marijuana as the Main Course

Most of the recipes in this book are for dessert dishes for a number of reasons. The first is because desserts, as a rule, have a high percentage of fat. This is the key ingredient that dissolves the drug glands on pot and is also responsible for its even distribution throughout the food.

The other reason is that it is easy to consume a small portion of a rich dessert. This small portion can easily contain all the drug desired.

When pot is added to the main course of a meal it usually comes on slower and less predictably. The amount of food eaten slows the assimilation of the drug, as does the content of the food. High carbohydrate recipes, such as pasta or pizza, will also slow the onset of the high. Even desserts spiked with marijuana will come on slower if eaten with a lot of other food.

For maximum effect marijuana should be eaten in a small amounts of food. Don't fret though, since appetite stimulation is often mentioned as one of the effects of marijuana, the munchies may well be part of the experience.

Slow assimilation of marijuana is not necessarily a bad thing - a medical user may look upon it as a "time release" dosage. It is a good way to take more of the drug and get less high. Getting high is sometimes an unwanted side effect to the medical user. For this person, adding pot to the main course can be beneficial.

People who want to get really high eating a full course dinner can always add a little more marijuana to the recipe. Even so, the high will come on some-

The amount of food eaten slows the assimilation of the drug, as does the content of the food.

what slower, and it may last for a longer period of time than if eaten on an empty stomach.

On the other hand, main courses made with milk or cheese, like macaroni and cheese, quiche or a grilled cheese sandwich, tend to be faster acting. Milk based sauces or gravies also come on fast. If you want to maximize the high with these foods, just don't eat a huge meal.

Marijuana butter and oil extracts can also easily be added to many prepared entrées, or drizzled on steamed vegetables. Just 1/2 teaspoon of these extracts are a moderate dose.

As noted above, lecithin is helpful in distributing the oils and THC evenly in foods. Add a little lecithin (with the marijuana and oil) to ready made soups, stews, or sauces.

Using Marijuana in Prepared Foods

Many people don't have the time, inclination, or equipment to prepare food from scratch. Fortunately, there are easy ways to add marijuana to many prepared foods. For example, marijuana leaf flour mixed with a little oil, can easily be added to canned soups, stews or gravies. Dosage is from 1/2 to 1 teaspoon per person. Up to 1/2 gram, if powdered sinsemilla flowers are used.

Most cake and cookie mixes call for added butter or shortening - this is an easy place to add the pot. Either leaf or bud flour can be whipped with butter or shortening and added to the mix. Five minutes with a electric mixer will make a smooth, easy-to-assimilate base.

You can use melted butter or oil, and marijuana leaf flour as a base to add to TV dinners and frozen meals. Any frozen entrée with some kind of sauce will do. Marijuana goes well with tomato, cheese, and meat dishes. It is easier to blend the marijuana into these frozen entrées if you defrost or partially cook them first. Dosage per person is 1/2 to 1 teaspoon.

For microwaveable entrées, cook for half the indicated time. Then stir in the pot, and finish cooking. There are all kinds of frozen "gourmet" entrées available, from macaroni and cheese to sirloin tips and vegetables. They are ready to slip into the microwave and nuke. Again, look for dishes with sauces. Just right for stoners on the go.

Marijuana leaf flour can also be added to prepared cookie dough sold ready to bake, wrapped in plastic rolls. To add marijuana leaf flour place 1/2 to 2 teaspoons per dose in a bowl, and knead the cookie dough into it, until thoroughly mixed. Reshape the dough into a roll, cut, and bake as directed. If you want to use powdered sinsemilla flowers, add up to 1/2 gram per cookie. (one cookie is one dose)

Canned frosting for cakes usually contains a lot of fat, which can easily act as the carrier for marijuana. Just mix marijuana leaf flour into it. Again use 1/2 to 1 teaspoons per dose.

Turning Down the Heat

High cooking temperatures can damage the cannabinoids, making for a less intense high. Most of the recipes in this book call for oven temperatures of 300° F or less. When adding marijuana to prepared foods or your own recipes, keep the temperature down. If you have to, cook foods for a longer time, rather than at a higher temperature.

Masking Odors and Colors

Cooking with marijuana, especially leaf, can cause odors. Most people would not recognize the smell as that of marijuana, but the aroma can be pungent. Keeping the heat down helps. But there other ways to disguise the scent of cooking marijuana.

Some flavor extracts, particularly orange extract, seem to neutralize odors. Just add a teaspoon to any cookie or cake recipe. Orange extract imparts a nice fruity flavor to baked goods, and is good with chocolate. Orange extract can also be used when making marijuana butter or oil.

Strong spices such as ginger, cinnamon, cloves, or nutmeg mask the smell of marijuana when making baked goods. A teaspoon in cookie recipes blends well with the taste of marijuana leaf. Chocolate also helps neutralize the smell of marijuana.

Recipes made with chocolate and marijuana leaf will not have the distinct green color of cakes and cookies made only with leaf. Chocolate baked goods look like regular confections, although they might have a greenish tinge if large amounts of leaf are used.

Main course recipes, or recipes where herbs are usually used, conceal the use of marijuana leaf pretty well. Tomato sauce or gravies made with leaf are discreet high foods, and the same is true of guacamole because it is green.

Cooks should use extra caution so that foods that don't obviously contain marijuana are not inadvertently consumed.

Utensils

A few utensils make cooking easier. The most important of these is the electric mixer. (The first step in most recipes is to beat the marijuana with the oil of the recipe. This step is very important. It helps break down the drug glands and makes them easy for the body to assimilate.) Five minutes with an electric mixer is worth about 20 with a wire whip, which can be used as an alternative. You can also use a rotary egg-beater or a blender if the recipe has enough liquid.

A sifter or sieve is the second important utensil. All grass going into a recipe should be sifted or screened to get out larger particles such as branches or stems.

Other useful devices include a coffee grinder, food processor and microwave oven. For making marijuana butter and oil (see page 22), a baby food sieve or potato ricer is helpful in squeezing the most out of the leaf. Although any steps can be done without these devices, they are great time savers.

Butter versus Margarine versus Oil

The recipes in this book call for the use of butter. This is a personal preference having to do with flavor. Margarine, shortening or oil can be used in place of butter in most recipes in this book. One pound of butter equals 2 cups of oil or shortening.

EQUIVALENTS

Fluids

3 teaspoons	= 1 tablespoon	= 15 milliliters
4 tablespoons	= 1/4 cup	= 60 ml
1 cup	= 8 fluid ounces	=.237 liters
2 cups	= 1 pint	= .473 liters
2 pints	= 1 quart	= .94 liters

Weights (approximate)

.25 ounces	= 7 grams
.5 ounces	= 14 grams
1 ounce	= 28 grams
16 ounces	= 1 pound
1 pound	= 454 grams
1000 grams	= 1 kilogram
1 kilogram	= 2.2 pounds
100 kilograms	= A federal rap

Volume (approximate)

1 cup	= 8 fluid ounces	= .24 liters
1 pint	= 16 fluid ounces	= .47 liters
1 quart	= 32 fluid ounces	= .94 liters
1 gallon	= 4 quarts	= 3.8 liters

Marijuana Flour (leaf or bud - powdered)

Weights/Volume (approximate)

1 teaspoon	= 1.8 grams	
1 tablespoon	= 5.5 grams	
1/4 cup	= 22.4 grams	
1/3 cup	= 28 grams	= 1 ounce
1/2 cup	= 45 grams	
2/3 cup	= 56 grams	= 2 ounces

Temperature

Fahrenheit	Centigrade
32	0
70	21
90	32
150	66
212	100
275	135
300	149
325	163
350	177
375	191
400	204

drinks

TEA N' TEA

Bring to a boil

  2 cups of water

  1 cup of milk or soy milk

  1-3 tablespoons marijuana leaf, or

    1-4 grams powdered sinsemilla flowers

Simmer 30 minutes or more.

Add and bring to boil

  6 cups of water

Turn off heat and add

  5 tea bags of your favorite tea*

Steep

Strain and Drink

  Yield: 9 cups

*Both herbal and caffeine-laced teas work well. Darjeeling, English and Irish Breakfast Teas are good choices for speed teas. Mint and/or chamomile are herbal favorites.

BHANG LASSI

In India marijuana leaves and milk are made into extracts known as Bhang. Bhang is often used to make delicious drinks with a kick, such as this traditional lassi.

On low heat mix together

  1 cup of low fat milk

  1-2 teaspoons marijuana leaf flour, or

    1/2-1 gram powdered sinsemilla flowers

  2 -3 tablespoons sugar

  1/2 teaspoon cardamon

  1 teaspoon rose water

  a dash of cinnamon, nutmeg or clove

Heat to near boiling. Simmer 30 minutes or more.

Cool and strain.

Mix in

  2 cups yogurt

  Yield: 2 servings

SALTY LASSI

Combine in a blender

  2 cups milk

  1 cup yogurt

  1/2 cup peeled cucumber

  1 stick of celery

  1/2 teaspoon black pepper

  1/2 teaspoon salt

  1-2 teaspoons marijuana leaf flour,

  or 1/2-1 gram powdered sinsemilla flowers

  1 teaspoon sugar

Blend until smooth.

Store cold for at least a couple of hours, preferably overnight.

Strain and drink.

  Serves 2

BUD WINE

To fortify wine add 1-3 grams of whole sinsemilla flowers to a quart of any wine with at least 10 per cent alcohol. Good with intense reds, like pinot or cabernet. Also good with fruity wines such as beaujolais, muscat, or even apple. Sherry is fine. One glass, please.

  Let age for 2-3 weeks.

  Serves 6

Use caution. Alcohol and pot are a strong mix.

HASH COFFEE

Dissolve .25-.5 gram of hashish in a cup of hot coffee. Add milk and sugar to taste.

EXTRACT DRINKS

Marijuana alcohol concentrate (see page 16) can be easily added to any coffee or tea drinks as well as smoothies or even a soda.

Use 1/2-1 teaspoon per dose.

FIRE WATER

Mix together all but one cup of a liter of your favorite hard liquor and 1-2 ounces of marijuana leaf. Cover and let sit for 1-3 days.

Strain the mixture through a sieve and press out any remaining liquid in the leaf. Pour the liquor that was set aside through the leaf and again press out any remaining liquid. If you use whole leaf you should be able to wring out remaining moisture by hand.

Strain through a coffee filter to remove any remaining particulate matter. Watch out, this stuff it is very potent. Up to 50 doses if 2 ounces of pot are used.

Variations:

1. Use up to 1 cup of sweet liquor (Kahlua is good) to sweeten the brew.

2. For a less green liquor, wash the leaf in tepid water, 90°F, for a few minutes to remove some of the chlorophyll in the leaf. If carefully washed, little THC will be lost. The leaf can be used wet but gently press out most of the water.

desserts

Cookies

GREENIES

Greenies are the basic, easy-to-make pot cookie. Not too sweet and very palatable.

oven 300° F (149° C)

Mix together

3/4 cup melted butter

3/4 cup milk or half & half

7 teaspoons-2/3 cup (.5-2 ounces) marijuana
   leaf flour*

1 egg

Beat for 5 minutes.

Mix in

3/4 cup sugar

1 teaspoon orange extract (optional)

1/2 teaspoon nutmeg (optional)

Sift in

1 teaspoon baking powder

2 cups flour

Beat with a mixer until thoroughly blended. Spoon onto greased cookie pans with a tablespoon.
Bake 25-30 minutes.

   Yield: 28 small cookies

Variations:

The recipe can be made with less sugar if desired and/or add up to 3/4 cup of chocolate chips, nuts or dried fruit.

*To make with marijuana flowers, see page 14. To make with marijuana butter or oil, see page 22.

NOTE RE: DOSAGE
ONE COOKIE = ONE
DOSE
Dosage is based on dividing each recipe into the yield quantity specified which varies from recipe to recipe.
Consistent baking practices will help in developing more accurate and desired potency.

Greenies—
ready to bake

EXTRACT COOKIES

oven 300° F (149° C)

Mix together

1/4-1/2 cup marijuana alcohol concentrate (See
page 18.)

3/4 cup softened butter

3/4 cup sugar

1/2 cup wheat germ

Sift in

1 teaspoon baking soda

2 cups flour

Beat until thoroughly mixed. Use a tablespoon to spoon onto an oiled cookie sheet. Bake for 20-30 minutes.

Yield: 25 cookies.

LEPRECHAUNS SHORTBREAD

oven 300 F (149° C)

Mix together

   1 cup softened butter or oil

   7 teaspoons-2/3 cup (.5-2 ounces) marijuana
      leaf flour*

   1 egg

   2 tablespoons Brandy (optional)

Beat for 5 minutes.

Add and mix

   3/4 cup brown sugar

   2 tablespoon molasses (optional)

   1 teaspoon vanilla

Sift in

   2 1/2 cups flour

   1 teaspoon baking powder

Beat until thoroughly mixed. Use a tablespoon to spoon onto an oiled cookie sheet. Bake for 20-30 minutes.

   Yield: 28 cookies

Variation: Add 1/2 cup chocolate chips or nuts.

*To make with marijuana flowers, see page 14. To make with marijuana butter or oil, see page 22.

LOADED PEANUT BUTTER COOKIES

oven 325° F (163° C)

Mix together

   2 cups peanut butter

   1 egg

   7 teaspoons-2/3 cup (.5-2 ounces) marijuana
      leaf flour*

Beat 5 minutes.

Add and mix in 3/4 cup brown sugar.

Sift in

   1 1/2 cup flour

   1 teaspoon baking powder

   2 tablespoons molasses

Beat until thoroughly mixed. Scoop cookie mix by the tablespoon on to cookie sheet. Bake for 20 minutes.

   Yield: 28 cookies

*To make with marijuana flowers, see page 14.

BUD'S SPICE COOKIES

oven 300° F (149° C)

Blend in a blender

  1/2 cup rum

  3-8 grams dried Sinsemilla flowers, cleaned of

    stem material

Mix together in a bowl

  blended mix above

  3/4 cup melted butter

  1 teaspoon ginger

  1/2 teaspoon cloves

  1/2 teaspoon cardamon

Beat 5 minutes.

Sift in

  2 1/2 cups flour

  1 teaspoon baking soda

Add

  1/2 cup raisins

Thoroughly mix. Use a tablespoon to spoon onto a cookie sheet. Bake for 20-30 minutes

  Yield: 20 cookies

MARY JANE'S VERY CHOCOLATE COOKIES

oven 300° F (149° C)

Beat together

  6 ounces bittersweet chocolate melted on

    low heat

  7 teaspoons-2/3 cups (.5-2 ounces) marijuana

    leaf flour*

  1/2 cup half & half

  1/2 cup melted butter

Add

  3/4 cup sugar

  2 tablespoons finely ground or instant coffee

Sift in and beat together

  1 1/2 cup flour

  1 teaspoon baking powder

Use a tablespoon to spoon onto a cooking sheet.

Bake for 20-30 minutes.

  Yield: 28 cookies

*to make with marijuana flowers, see page 14.

PUFF'S BROWNIES

oven 325° F (163° C)

Beat together

6 ounces semisweet chocolate melted on very
low heat

1/2 cup softened butter

4 teaspoons to 1/3 cup (.3-1 ounce) marijuana
leaf flour*

1 egg

a dash of salt

2 teaspoons vanilla

3/4 cup sugar

Beat 5 minutes.

Sift in

1/2 cup flour

1 teaspoon baking powder

Add

1/2 cup chopped nuts (optional)

When thoroughly mixed, spread on oiled baking pan.

Bake for 25-30 minutes.

Yield: 14 brownies

*To make with marijuana flowers, see page 14. *To
make with marijuana butter or oil, see page 22.

WILD OAT COOKIES

oven 325° F (163° C)

Beat well

2 eggs

Beat in

1 cup sugar

3 tablespoons melted butter or oil

7 teaspoons-2/3 cup (.5 to 2 ounces) marijuana
leaf flour*

2 teaspoons vanilla

1 teaspoon salt

Stir in

2 cups oatmeal

Thoroughly mix. Spoon on to a cookie sheet by the
tablespoon. Bake 15-20 minutes.

Yield: 28 cookies

*To make with marijuana flowers, see page 14.

Cakes, Frostings, Muffins and Sweet Breads

HAMMER CAKE

oven to 325° F (163° C)

Beat together

1 cup softened butter

1/6-1/3 cup (.5-1 ounce) marijuana leaf flour*

3/4 cup sugar

1/2 cup orange juice

1/2 cup half & half

3 eggs

Sift in

2 cups flour

2 teaspoons baking powder

When thoroughly mixed, pour into an oiled baking pan. Bake for 45 minutes to 1 hour.

Yield: 16 slices

*To make with marijuana flowers, see page 14. To make with marijuana butter or oil, see page 22.

STONEY HEMP CARROT CAKE

oven 325° F(163° C)

Beat together

3/4 cup softened butter

2 tablespoons-1/4 cup (.4-.8 ounce) marijuana leaf flour*

Add and beat

1 cup finely grated carrot

3/4 cup brown sugar

3/4 cup milk

2 eggs

1/2 cup shredded coconut

1 teaspoon grated orange peel

1 teaspoon ginger

Sift in

1 3/4 cups flour

1/8 cup finely ground hemp seed (use a coffee grinder)

1 tablespoon baking powder

When thoroughly mixed pour into an oiled 9" x 12" baking pan. Bake for about 45 minutes.

Yield: 16 slices

*To make with marijuana flowers, see page 14. To make with marijuana butter or oil, see page 22.

SPACE CAKE

oven 325° F (163° C)

Beat together

  1 cup softened butter

  1/6 to 1/3 cup (.5 to 1 ounce) marijuana leaf
    flour*

  3 tablespoons brandy or coffee liquor

  1/2 cup half & half

  6 ounces bittersweet chocolate melted on
    very low heat

Add and mix

  3/4 cup sugar

  2 teaspoons vanilla

  3 eggs

Sift in

  2 1/2 cups flour

  2 teaspoons baking powder

Thoroughly mix then pour into 2 oiled 9" cake pans. Bake for about 20 minutes. When done, let cool thoroughly, then fill and frost as for layer cakes.

Spread 1/2 cup raspberry preserves between the layers and use the frosting below.

Yield: 14 or more slices

  Variations: Several Marijuana cooks swear by ready made Chocolate Cake Mix. Just add an extra egg to make the cake more moist.

*To make with marijuana flowers, see page 14. To make with marijuana butter or oil, see page 22.

SUZY'S CREAM CHEESE FROSTING

Good general purpose frosting.

Whip together with an electric mixer

  1/2 cup cream cheese (low fat is okay)

  1/4 cup powdered sugar

  1 tablespoon milk or yogurt

Whip until smooth and spread on the space or carrot cake.

Not psychoactive.

Variation:

SUZY TAKES A TRIP FROSTING

Add 1-3 tablespoons of Marijuana leaf flour or 2-5 grams powdered Sinsemilla flowers to the frosting above, and one tablespoon more of milk. Blend until smooth. This frosting can be spread on any packaged cake or muffin, making them "high" food.

Yield: 10 doses

DO NOT spread this psychoactive frosting on any of the psychoactive cakes and muffins in this book.

MARIJUANA BUTTER FROSTING

Whip together with an electric mixer

1/8-1/4 cup softened marijuana butter
   (See page 22)

1/4 cup softened butter

1/4 cup powdered sugar

1 tablespoon milk or yogurt

Spread on ready made cakes and muffins. DO NOT use on any of the psychoactive recipes in this book.

Yield: 8 doses

MYSTIC MUFFINS

oven 300° F (149° C)

Whip together

1 tablespoon-1/4 cup (.2-.8 ounces)
   marijuana leaf flour*

1/2 cup melted butter or oil

Add

1/2 cup orange juice

1 cup milk

3/4 cup sugar

Sift in and mix

2 1/2 cup flour

3 teaspoons baking powder

Stir in

1/2 cup blueberries or nuts

Spoon into an oiled muffin tin and bake for 20 minutes.

Yield: 12 muffins.

*To make with marijuana flowers, see page 14. To make with marijuana butter or oil, see page 22.

GOING BANANAS BREAD

oven 325° F (163° C)

Beat together

  1/2 cup oil or butter

  2 tablespoons-1/4 cup (.4-.8 ounce)
    marijuana leaf flour*

Add and beat

  3 cut-up bananas

  1 egg

  1/2 cup sugar

  1/2 cup of milk

Sift in

  2 cups flour

  1 teaspoon baking powder

Add

  1/2 cup chopped nuts (optional)

When thoroughly mixed, pour into an oiled bread
pan. Bake for 45-60 minutes.

  Yield: 16 slices

*To make with marijuana flowers, see page 14. To
make with marijuana butter or oil, see page 22.

Puddings Candies & Ice Cream

MARIJUANA BUTTER AKA "KILLER" FUDGE

Melt and mix on low heat or in a double boiler

  1/4-1/2 cup marijuana butter (see page 22)

  10 ounces bittersweet or milk chocolate

  1 cup sugar

  1/2 cup half & half or milk

  1/4 cup cocoa

  1/4 cup chopped nuts

Spread on a shallow baking pan and cool, then cut.

  Yield: 14 squares

MILE HIGH CHOCOLATE PUDDING

Mix together

  1/4 cup water

  3 tablespoons of corn starch

Set aside.

Whisk together in a sauce pan

  1 egg (optional)

  2 cups milk or soy milk

  1-4 teaspoons of marijuana leaf flour or

    .5- 2 grams of sinsemilla flowers

  3 tablespoons sugar

  6 tablespoons cocoa

Heat on low, stirring occasionally, to keep it from sticking to the bottom of the pan. Just before the mix boils, stir the corn starch and water and pour it into the mixture, stirring quickly until the mixture thickens. Serve hot or cold.

Because of the lecithin in the milk or soy milk, pudding is one of the fastest acting psychoactive desserts.

Makes 4 1/2 cup servings

Variation: Any instant pudding that is heated and uses milk can be used to make a high dessert. Follow the directions on the box for making it. Add marijuana leaf flour at a dosage of 1/2-1 teaspoon per person.

HEAD CHOCOLATES

Mix In

1 pound (454 grams) bittersweet or milk chocolate melted on a very low heat or in a double boiler

7 teaspoons-2/3 cup (.5-2 ounces) marijuana leaf flour

1/4 cup melted butter

1/4 cup milk or half & half

Thoroughly mix and heat (low) for 5 minutes. Cut squares of aluminum foil to receive tablespoons of the mix. Cool until hardened, then consume. Refrigerate any that are left.

Yield: 28 chocolates

Variation 1: To use sinsemilla flowers in this recipe add 3.5-14 grams of powdered flowers. Add as you would the leaf. Take out the melted butter.

Variation 2: Filled Chocolates

Any fruit preserve (raspberry is especially good) can be encapsulated in the chocolate. To do this spread a thin layer of the melted chocolate on the aluminum foil with a tablespoon. Then put a dab of preserves in the center of the chocolate with a teaspoon. Finally spread a layer of chocolate over the preserves.

Variation 3: Add 1/2 cup of chopped nuts or raisins to the melted chocolate.

EXTRACT CHOCOLATES

Add to a sauce pan on low heat or in a double boiler and mix until melted

   1 pound milk chocolate

   2 tablespoons-1/4 cup marijuana alcohol
     concentrate (see page 18)

When melted and thoroughly mixed, use a tablespoon to spoon on to squares of aluminum foil.

   Yield: 25-30 chocolates

POT ICE CREAM

You need an ice cream maker for this recipe.

Heat together, slowly

   2 teaspoons-3 tablespoons (4-16 grams)
     marijuana leaf flour or 1-4 grams powdered
     sinsemilla flowers

   3 tablespoons brandy

   1 cup heavy cream

   2 tablespoons vanilla

   3/4 cup sugar

Heat 20 minutes. Do not boil. Remove from heat.

Mix together in a separate pan,

   2 cups milk

   2 eggs

Combine all ingredients and freeze in an ice cream freezer.

   Yield: 8 servings (approximately 1 quart)

Variations

1. Substitute 1-4 tablespoons marijuana alcohol concentrate (see page 18) for the brandy and marijuana flour.

2. For chocolate ice cream add 8 ounces semisweet chocolate when the ingredients are heated.

CANDIED SINSE FLOWERS

This works best with flowers that are a little airy rather than tight.

Spray PAM (sprayable cooking oil) lightly on sinsemilla flowers.

Bake in a pre-heated oven 400° F (204° C) for 5 minutes. Cool on a wire rack.

Mix and heat in a separate pan

I cup sugar

I teaspoon molasses (optional)

1/8 cup water

Heat until the mix is a smooth syrup. Dunk the buds briefly in the syrup. Remove excess and return to wire rack until the syrup hardens.

Dosage: 1/4-1/2 gram per person

Variation:

CHOCOLATE CANDIED SINSE FLOWERS

Bake the bud as explained above. Instead of the sugar syrup, melt 3 ounces of bittersweet chocolate on low heat. Dip the flowers briefly in the chocolate, shake off excess, return to rack to harden.

m a i n   d i s h e s

Appetizers

BLAZED GUACAMOLE

Avocados are a good vegetable to use with pot
because they contain 15% or more oil.

Mash together

 2 avocados

 1-4 teaspoons marijuana leaf flour

  or 1/2-2 grams powdered sinsemilla flowers

 2 tablespoons sour cream

 1 clove minced garlic

 dash salt and tabasco

Refrigerate covered for 2 hours or more.

Serve with corn chips and salsa.

 Yield: 4 servings

Variation: To make with marijuana oil (see page 22)
use 1-4 teaspoons. Omit the sour cream.

POT STICKERS

You will need one package prepared wonton shells,
at least 20 pieces.

Combine

 1/2 pound (227 grams) ground beef, pork or

  chicken

 3 tablespoons-1/3 cup (1 ounce) marijuana leaf

 flowers or 3-8 grams powdered sinsemilla

  flowers

 1 tablespoon sesame oil

 1/4 pound finely chopped shrimp

 2 tablespoon sherry or brandy

 1 tablespoon cornstarch

 3 tablespoons finely chopped onion

 3 tablespoons finely chopped fresh parsley or

  cilantro

 3 tablespoons chopped bamboo shoots

 2 teaspoons soy sauce

 1/2 teaspoon pepper

 1/2 teaspoon grated orange peel

When all ingredients are thoroughly mixed, spoon by the tablespoon into the wonton. Shape like a pot sticker and seal the end of the wonton. Use a vegetable steamer to steam the dumplings for 30 minutes. Serve with plum sauce or vinegar.

Yield: 20 servings

Casseroles and Potpies

HEMP SEED VEGGIE CASSEROLE

oven to 325°F (163°C)

Mix together

  1/2 cup hemp seed ground finely in a coffee
    grinder

  1 1/2 cooked brown rice

  1/2 cup of each cooked and chopped

  carrots, potatoes, onions and green beans

  1 egg

  1 clove crushed garlic

  1 teaspoon salt

  1 teaspoon pepper

  1/2 cup grated sharp cheddar

  1/2 cup milk or yogurt

  1/4 cup wine or fruit juice

Combine all ingredients in a mixing bowl then turn
    onto an oiled casserole dish.

Bake for 30-40 minutes.

  Yield: 6 servings

Not psychoactive.

CASSEROLE SAUCE

Melt and mix

  2 tablespoons butter

  2 tablespoons flour

  salt and pepper

Stir in

  1 cup milk

Heat slowly and stir until sauce thickens.

Stir in

  2 tablespoons white wine

Remove from heat.

Pour over the cooked Hemp Seed Casserole.

Variation:

HIGH HEMP LOAVES

The place to add the pot to the hemp recipe above is in the sauce.

Add one of the following:

  2 teaspoons-2 tablespoons (4-10 grams)
    marijuana leaf flour

  1 to 3 grams powdered sinsemilla flowers

  1 to 2 tablespoons of marijuana butter or oil
    (See page 22.)

Cook as described above.

CHICKEN POT PIE

oven 350° F (177° C)

Combine in a skillet on low heat

  2 tablespoons butter

  1 tablespoon flour

  2-5 teaspoons marijuana leaf flour or

    1-3 grams of powdered sinsemilla flowers

Cook on low a few minutes. Set aside.

Combine in a pot

  1 cup water or stock

  1 1/2 cups chicken

  1 large diced potato

  1/2 cup finely diced onion

  2 cups diced veggies

  1/4 cup wine

  1 tablespoon soy sauce

  1/2 teaspoon black pepper

  1/2 teaspoon sage

  1/2 teaspoon rosemary

Simmer for 20 minutes, until the potatoes are done, then stir in the butter, pot mixture, with a wire

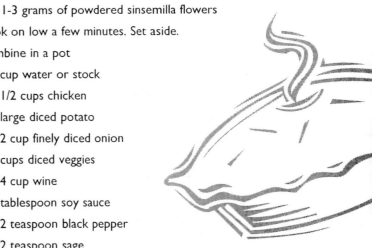

whisk. Thoroughly mix. Continue to cook until the mixture is thickened. Remove from heat. Pour into a 9" casserole or pie plate.

Cover with a prepared pie crust , or roll your own. Bake at 350° F (177° C) for 20-30 minutes, until crust is brown.

Yield: 4 servings

Variation 1: To use marijuana butter or oil (see page 22), use 2-5 teaspoons. Combine with 3 tablespoons of flour. No reason to heat it, just stir it in as you would the leaf flour and butter.

Variation 2: Use puff pastry shells. Cook as directed. Spoon the Pot Pie mixture into them.

Variation 3: Forget the crust, add 1/2 cup water, simmer the mixture another 10 minutes, and eat it as a stew.

PIE CRUST

Combine

1 stick softened butter (1/2 cup)

1 cup flour

Roll out with a rolling pin to fit pie.

Not psychoactive.

Pasta and Pizza

POTARONI AND CHEESE

oven 300° F (149° C)

Undercook (al dente)

12 ounce of macaroni

Set aside in a casserole dish.

Combine with a wire whisk in a sauce pan,

4 cups low fat milk

1 egg (optional)

3 tablespoons cornstarch (mix with a little
milk first)

2 teaspoons sugar

1 teaspoon pepper

1/2 cup wine

Heat to near boiling stirring occasionally.

Add

1-2 cups of cubed sharp cheese

1-3 tablespoons marijuana leaf flour or
2-4 grams powdered sinsemilla flowers

Stir until smooth then pour over the macaroni.
Sprinkle with bread crumbs. Bake for 30 minutes.
Unlike some main dishes Potaroni comes on fast.

Yield: 9 servings

Variation: To make with marijuana butter or oil (see
page 22), use 1-3 tablespoons. Add at the same time
as the cheese.

PSYCHIC SPAGHETTI SAUCE

Combine in a sauce pan on very low heat,

3 tablespoons olive oil

4-6 cloves minced garlic

1 finely chopped onion

Saute 5 minutes. Do not brown.

Add

1-3 tablespoons marijuana leaf flour
or 2-4 grams powdered sinsemilla flowers

Saute another minute.

Turn up heat.

Add

1 can crushed tomatoes (28 ounces)

1-2 teaspoons sugar

1 tablespoon soy sauce

2 teaspoons powdered oregano

1 teaspoon sage

1/2 teaspoon pepper

2 tablespoons red wine

Bring to boil. Lower heat and simmer at least 1 hour. Serve with pasta of your choice.

Yield: 6 servings

Variations

1. Veggie sauce: Add a couple of cups of diced celery and carrots. When they are cooked puree the sauce in a blender.

2. Meat sauce: Cook 1/2 pound cooked ground beef. Pour off excess fat. Add to the sauce and let simmer.

3. Aztec Sauce: Add 4 ounces of semisweet chocolate to the sauce.

4. Sauce In A Jar: Forget the gourmet approach, and go for the Ragu. The leaf flour can be added directly to prepared tomato sauce with meat. For vegetarian sauces saute the marijuana leaf flour with a couple of tablespoons of oil, then add to the sauce.

Dosage: 1/2-1 teaspoon per person

PARA-NORMAL PIZZA

While the sauce above is simmering make a pizza dough. Prepared pizza crusts also work well.

YOUR OWN DOUGH

Combine in a mixing bowl

1 1/2 cup warm water, 90°F (42° C)

1 teaspoon sugar

1 package of baker's yeast

Let stand 5 minutes while yeast works.

Stir in with a wire whip

1 cup of flour

1/4 cup wheat germ or hemp seed meal

Knead in by hand

2 1/2 cups flour

2 tablespoons olive oil

Cover and let the dough rise approximately
15 minutes in a warm place.

Dust the dough with flour and knead again. Then use
a rolling pin to shape the dough into 2 pizza crusts.

Put on an oiled baking pan

Cover the dough with the sauce up to 1/4 inch from
the edge.

Top with

8 ounces grated mozzarella cheese

2 ounces grated imported provolone or other
sharp cheese

1 teaspoon marijuana leaf flour

or 1 gram powdered sinsemilla flowers

Add other toppings to taste. Less cheese can be
used if desired.

Bake at 400° F (204° C) for 15-20 minutes.

Yield: 8 servings

Variation 1: Adding Pot To Frozen Pizza.

Mix 1-4 teaspoons of marijuana leaf flour or 1-2
grams powdered sinsemilla flowers with 2 tablespoons of oil. Spread the mixture evenly over your
favorite frozen pizza. Cook as directed.

Yield: 4 servings

Variation 2: Adding marijuana oil (see page 22) to
delivered or frozen Pizza.

Evenly brush on 1-4 teaspoons. Consume.

Yield: 4 servings

WEED PESTO

Grind in a food processor

   1 1/2 cups fresh basil leaves

   2 cloves garlic

   1/4 cup pine or other nuts

Process until the mix is thoroughly pureed.

Put in a bowl and add

   1/4 cup finely grated parmesan cheese

   2-6 teaspoons (4-10 grams) marijuana leaf flour

      or 1-3 grams powdered sinsemilla flowers

   3 tablespoons olive oil

   2 tablespoons sour cream or yogurt

Thoroughly combine all ingredients. Store for an hour or so before using. Heat up just before use. Good on pasta, or it can be added to soup, potatoes or other vegetables.

   Yield: 6 servings

Vegetables

HALF BAKED BEANS

Combine in a skillet on low heat

   2 tablespoons oil

   1-2 tablespoon marijuana leaf flour

      or 1 1/2-3 grams powdered sinsemilla flowers

   4 cloves crushed garlic

Cook on low heat until garlic wilts. Do not brown.

Add

   1 pound canned baked beans or beans in

      tomato sauce

   2 tablespoons barbecue sauce

   1/2 teaspoon tabasco

   1/2 teaspoon cinnamon

   1/2 teaspoon nutmeg

   1/4 teaspoon cloves

Simmer until the beans and sauce are at the desired thickness.

   Yield: 6 servings

Variation: Use 1-2 tablespoons of marijuana oil (see page 22) instead of the leaf or flowers. Keep the heat low.

BLUNTED TOFU & VEGGIES

Cook 1 cup brown rice. Set aside.

Combine in a skillet or wok on medium heat

   1 clove minced garlic

   2 tablespoons of oil

   1/2 cup cubed tofu

Cook until the tofu is lightly browned.

Stir in

   1-2 teaspoons marijuana leaf flour

     or 1/2-1 grams powdered sinsemilla flowers

Add

   3 cups of mixed vegetables

   2 tablespoons wine

    or 1 tablespoon vinegar

   1/2 teaspoon black pepper

   1-2 teaspoons soy sauce

   1 teaspoon corn starch

Stir until all ingredients are coated and cooked..

Serve over rice.

   Yield: 2 servings

sauces, gravies and salad dressings

REEFER GRAVY

Combine

 2 tablespoons corn starch

 3 tablespoons water

Set aside

Heat together in a large frying pan

 3 tablespoons butter, oil or drippings from a roast

 1 tablespoon flour

 2-6 teaspoons (4-10 grams) marijuana leaf flour

 or 1-3 grams powdered sinsemilla flowers

 1 tablespoon soy sauce

 1 cup wine

 1 cup stock or water and bullion cube

 1/2 teaspoon pepper

 1 teaspoon sugar

Heat slowly until near boiling, stirring frequently with

 a wire whip.

Add the cornstarch and water. Stir until it thickens.

 Yield: 6 servings

Variation: To use marijuana butter or oil (see page 21) in place of the grass, use 3-6 teaspoons. Reduce the amount of regular butter, if you want to.

HOLLAND DAZE SAUCE

Beat together with a wire whip

 1 egg

 1/4 cup half & half

 1 teaspoon corn starch

 1 teaspoon sugar

 2 tablespoons wine or lemon juice

 a dash of nutmeg, cardamon and/or tabasco

 salt and pepper to taste

Melt in a small frying or saute pan

  2 tablespoons butter

Add

  1/2-2 teaspoons marijuana leaf flour

    or 1/4-1 gram powdered sinsemilla flowers

Saute the pot and butter for a couple of minutes on low heat.

Add the mixture above. Cook on low heat until near boiling, when the sauce will thicken. Use immediately on eggs or over cooked vegetables or potatoes.

  Yield: 2 servings

Variation 1: Melt in up to 1/4 cup sharp cheese

Variation 2: Use 1-2 teaspoons of marijuana butter or oil (see page 21) in place of the grass.

PSYCHEDELIC SALAD DRESSING

Combine in a Jar

  1/4 cup olive oil

  1 small clove minced garlic

  1-3 teaspoons marijuana leaf flour

    or 1-2 grams powdered sinsemilla flowers

  2 tablespoon wine

  3 tablespoons balsamic vinegar

  2 tablespoons water

  2 teaspoons soy sauce

  1 teaspoon sugar or ketchup

  pepper to taste

  1/2 teaspoon lecithin

Combine and shake up all ingredients. For best results let sit for an hour or two. Pour over a large salad. Use bread to sop up excess dressing.

  Yield: 4 servings

miscellaneous yummies

LUNAR PANCAKES

Beat together

    2 tablespoons melted butter or oil

    4 teaspoons to 3 tablespoons (7-16 grams)
        marijuana leaf flour or 2-4 grams powdered
        sinsemilla flowers

    1/2 cup milk or soy milk

    1/2 cup half & half

    1 teaspoon vanilla

    2 eggs

Mix in

    2 tablespoons sugar

    1 1/2 cup flour

    1/2 cup blueberries or other fruit (optional)

    1 teaspoon baking powder

Cook on griddle or fry pan, oil the pan for the first batch. Cook on medium heat, until bubbles form on the top of the cake. Then turn and cook until browned. Good hot or cool. Use the lower amounts of pot if you are going to eat more than one. Seem to get more potent as they sit.

   Yield: 12 pancakes

Variation 1: To make with marijuana butter or oil (see page 21) use 2-4 tablespoons in place of the grass. Take out the regular butter.

Variation 2: This recipe will work with most pancake mixes. Use the mix in place of flour and proceed as above. Pancake mixes are often sweetened and contain baking powder, so you can cut back these ingredients.

GRILLED CHEESE AND HERB PESTO SANDWICH

Mix together

  1/2-1 teaspoon marijuana leaf flour

    or .25-.5 gram powdered sinsemilla flowers

  1 teaspoon olive oil

  small amount of finely minced garlic

Make a sandwich with

  2 pieces bread

  2 thin slices of cheese

  Thin tomato slices (optional)

  The pesto mix above

Spread the pot and oil between the two slices of cheese with the tomato next to the bread. Grill in a pat of butter until cheese inside the sandwich is melted and the bread is grilled brown. Use low to moderate heat and a weight (pan with water) to hold the sandwich against the pan.

  Yield: 1 sandwich

POT YOGURT

Yogurt makers were such a fad that they turn up at nearly every garage sale. The heating of milk as done in making yogurt is also a perfect method for preparing marijuana to be consumed. Marijuana prepared in this way comes on fast with a good clean high. Dosage per person is 1/2-1 teaspoon of marijuana leaf flour. You can also use marijuana oil (see page 21) at 1/2-1 teaspoon per dose or .25-.5 grams powdered sinsemilla flowers per dose in yogurt.

Yogurt makers usually make 4 cups, so stir together 1 quart of milk and 2-4 teaspoons marijuana leaf flour. To make yogurt you also have to add a couple tablespoons of yogurt containing active yogurt cultures (check the label) for starter. Add up to 2 tablespoons of sugar if desired and thoroughly mix. Pour into the yogurt cups and turn the machine on.

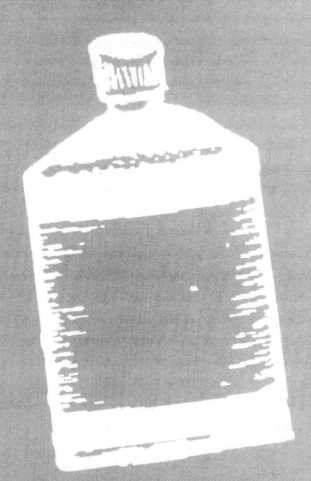

Medicine

marijuana for medicine and health

Besides being one of the most popular recreational drugs, marijuana has been used for centuries as a medicinal plant. It is one of the primary herbs in both Chinese and Indian (Ayurvedic) medicine, where it is used to treat appetite disorders, arthritis & rheumatism, menstrual cramping, insomnia, and depression. Written references to cannabis as a healing plant date back at least 4000 years. In spite of this, marijuana is seldom mentioned in modern books and writings on herbal medicines.

In 1937 pot prohibition put an end to the use of cannabis as an accepted medicine in this country, but its use was declining even before it was made illegal. This is because the drug companies, at the turn of the century, could not separate the 60 cannabinoids which the plant may contain. They were thus unable to produce cannabis drugs which were standardized in effect. Unlike opium poppies, from which several drugs like morphine, codeine or heroin were isolated and reliably produced, cannabis preparations remained variable. Western medicine favors drug agents that can be easily targeted for specific illnesses. Since the cannabis preparations were variable, they were prescribed less.

The quality of the cannabis drug depended on the plant from which it was derived, and cannabis has a large gene pool. Each batch of medicine could have different properties than the last.

In 1964, when THC was first synthesized, the possibility of targeting various cannabinoids of the Cannabis plant to specific illnesses opened up. The "drug war" has up to now kept a lid on this possibility. The only cannabis-like drug available in the U.S.A.

Written references to cannabis as a healing plant date back at least 4000 years.

is Marinol (Dronabinol), which is synthesized delta 9 THC in sesame oil. Though this cannabinoid is the most active in getting people high, marijuana may contain many other cannabinoids, many of which may modify the high, or have medicinal value.

Though marijuana's use as a medicine is almost totally prohibited in the U.S., groups of people with certain illnesses have been using the drug illicitly. Many of these people are in desperate circumstances, such as being treated for cancer or HIV infection.

Many patients have petitioned the government for access to pot. Despite the fact that many of these people are in intractable pain, at present, only 9 people in the United States receive marijuana legally from the government for medical purposes.

The history of the federal governments response to pleas for medical marijuana have been particularly cruel. NORML (National Organization for the Reform of Marijuana Laws) began petitioning the government to furnish medical marijuana in 1975. Their lawsuit also attempted to stop the government from interfering in medical research, by getting marijuana reclassified under law. It is presently a Schedule 1 drug which, in legal terms, means it has no medical value and a high potential for abuse.

It took NORML, and other interested parties, 11 years to get a hearing on this matter before the Drug Enforcement Administration, the DEA. Strangely enough, the DEA's administrative law judge Francis J. Young, after hearing all the evidence, found in favor of NORML and called marijuana, in its natural form, one of the safest therapeutically active substances known to man. Judge Young recommended that marijuana be reclassified. This ruling was not enough to stop the DEA's "reefer madness" attitude: they simply refused to do as the judge recommended.

Many states have passed laws to allow medical marijuana, at least in a limited way, for cancer chemotherapy and radiation patients, many of whom find that marijuana is the only drug that effectively combats the nausea associated with these procedures.

As of 1994, 37 states have passed such laws. Despite the fact that these laws were passed to help the very sickest patients, the DEA's response continues to be totally obstructionist. Very few of the sick ever got their medicine, at least legally.

Even when another government agency, in this case the Food And Drug Administration, interceded on behalf of a few dying people, the DEA has been intractable. Though more than two dozen "compassionate use" petitions have been approved by the FDA, the DEA simply refused to supply the pot or erected new roadblocks to prevent people from getting the medicine.

The Brownie Mary case in San Francisco shows how the laws against medical marijuana might soon fade away. Charged with felony possession of marijuana for sale, because she was busted baking marijuana cookies for AIDS patients, Mary fought the charges. All charges were eventually dropped after the San Francisco Board of Supervisors declared August 25, 1992 "Brownie Mary Day" and commended her publicly for her work with AIDS patients. Eighty percent of San Franciscans had recently voted for making medical marijuana legal.

AIDS and Cancer patients in San Francisco have since formed a buyers club whose purpose is to supply marijuana to people who need it medically. Though the club has garnered much publicity and the authorities know what is going on they have not yet moved against it.

In fact, many city officials have made statements favorable to the aim of the club, delivering medicine to the sick. It is not known what, if anything, the federal government intends to do about the club.

There are humans in pain behind all the pot that was denied and the lawsuits that have been filed. Many of these people lived shorter lives and died in pain because they did not have access to medical marijuana.

Ultimately, it will be untenable to legalize the medical, but maintain the prohibition against the recreational use of marijuana. Are recreational users just having fun, or are they "self medicating"?

This debate is yet to start, but it should prove to be illuminating. As the hippies move into old age they may look to marijuana more for its medicinal qualities rather than getting high. Young and old may be united looking for relief in this workaday world.

Using Medically

Up to now most illnesses treated with marijuana have been with smoked marijuana. There are many distinct differences between smoking or using cooked marijuana.

The biggest difference is in how long the high lasts. When pot is eaten the psychoactive effects may last 5 to 8 hours, the herb's medicinal effects may last up to 12 hours. Medically, marijuana has to be taken less often when eaten.

Eating cooked marijuana is also more effective than

smoking for painful conditions. When smoked, marijuana does have some pain relieving qualities, but for the most part, these are related to relieving tension.

When eaten, however, cannabis has very strong analgesic and anti-inflammatory effects.

It is beyond the scope of this book to prescribe marijuana for any specific ailment. However, cannabis is presently being used for relief from many chronic conditions. Some are well documented and we have listed them.

Other information is anecdotal, but comes from people actually treating their illness with this drug. Much more research needs to be done in this area but sadly, even if the research is allowed, it will probably be done to create costly patented medicines.

Marinol

Marinol is the trade name for the one Cannabis-like drug (Dronabinol) approved by the Food and Drug Administration. It contains synthetic delta 9 THC in a sesame oil base. Because it is patented, the drug is quite expensive, up to $25 a day, as prescribed.

It is presently approved, in a limited way, for use in cancer, AIDS, and some eating disorders.

Many people who have used Marinol claim that marijuana, the herb, is more effective. There have also been many complaints that Marinol is anxiety producing. This may be because of the lack of other cannabinoids in the drug, some of which have been shown to relieve anxiety. Marijuana is a complex drug, while Marinol contains a single medicinal agent. Claims, by the medical community, that Marinol does not get you high are clearly wrong. Remember, Marinol contains THC, the most active cannabinoid in getting "high". Reports of not getting high are related to dose, as Marinol contains a very small amount of THC. Higher doses of Marinol definitely get people high.

Though Marinol is at least somewhat effective in stimulating appetite, the use for which it is approved, it is likely that a drug containing multiple cannabinoids would be more therapeutic. This accounts for reports that the herb itself is superior to Marinol in creating "the munchies".

That said, the availability of Marinol should be expanded. As it is, just one patented process of synthesizing THC has been approved. This has given the drug company making Marinol an exorbitant profit. Even in the small doses prescribed the drug can cost $600-$800 dollars a month. Other methods of synthesizing THC are not under patent and could be used inexpensively.

Opening up the illnesses treated with Marinol could answer a lot of questions relating to the specific action of THC in suppressing disease. If the drug were approved for the treatment of Multiple Sclerosis or Rheumatoid Arthritis, for example, we should be able to gauge if it is THC which is primarily responsible for giving relief from these illnesses. If not, medicines containing other cannabinoids could be devised.

Considering the number of cannabinoids marijuana contains, it seems likely that many pharmaceutical drugs could be developed from the plant. For the most part research has been inhibited because marijuana remains illegal, and any research done with the drug is mired in red tape. It took 30 years to get Marinol on the market from the first synthesis of THC in 1964. And this is only one of the 60 cannabinoids the plant may contain.

It is very easy to make marinol-like drugs by making homemade capsules containing either leaf or flowers (see below). Both have a full complement of cannabinoids. They can also be quite inexpensive to make if marijuana leaf is used.

I urge people contemplating using Cannabis medicinally to seek unbiased medical help. If that is not possible seek information from other people using it. Marijuana is a safe drug. But for new users especially, be cautious with dosage until you are sure of the effects. Please don't stop taking prescribed medication without consulting a doctor. Books like *Marijuana, The Forbidden Medicine* by Lester Grinspoon (Yale Press) are the most up to date source on using marijuana medicinally.

Capsules

As marijuana becomes more popular as a medicine, it seems natural that capsules filled with pot have become popular. Gelatin capsules and capsule makers are sold in many health food stores.

Two sizes of capsules and capsule makers are usually available, the 0 and 00 sizes. The 0 size holds .2 grams of marijuana when thoroughly filled. The 00 size holds .4 grams. Keep in mind the 00 size capsule may be a little large for some people to swallow. If so, use the 0 size.

Capsules can be made using both marijuana leaf flour and bud. Either way, oil must be used to prepare the pot. Without oil the drug glands on pot will break down slowly during digestion. Unless it is processed, the pot will be absorbed slowly and unpredictably.

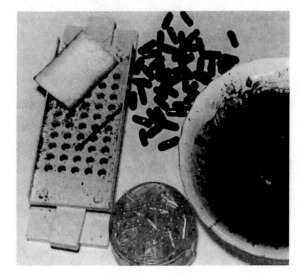

The oil also facilitates the absorption of marijuana's active cannabinoids into the bloodstream.

Untreated pot can also irritate the stomach. This is not from the THC glands, but from the sharp cystolith hairs found on both bud and leaf. (See page 4.) The oil and a little heat helps to soften these hairs.

Any good oil, such as olive or canola, can be used in making capsules. Medicinal oils such as hemp and flax oils can also be used, if you keep heating to a minimum. Alcohol should not be used capsule making, as the alcohol will dissolve the gelatin capsules.

Capsules From Marijuana Leaf Flour

To be processed for capsules marijuana leaf flour (see page 12) must be thoroughly mixed with small amounts of oil. The pot must be thoroughly coated, but flaky enough to fit through the holes of a capsule maker. Use 3 tablespoons of oil per ounce (1/3 cup) of marijuana leaf flour.

Put the leaf flour in a small frying pan, pour the oil over the pot, and thoroughly mix with a fork. Saute the pot on a low flame for a few minutes, stirring the pot so that it is evenly heated. When cooled the pot is ready for the capsules.

Capsule makers make 50 capsules at a time. The bottom of the capsule fits through holes in the deck of the capsule maker, and the herb is pushed over the deck into the capsules. The pot mix then needs to be tamped into the capsules, until they are thoroughly filled. The head of a nail is a good tool for tamping the cannabis into the caps. You may have to fill and tamp 2 or 3 times before the capsules are filled.

Two 00 capsules filled with marijuana leaf flour is about .8 grams, a moderate to average dose. One capsule will not get most people high, but will have medicinal qualities such as appetite stimulation.

The capsules will keep for a couple of weeks at room temperature. For freshness, however, they should be refrigerated. They will keep a month or more. Capsules can be kept at least 6 months in the freezer. Condensation as they defrost may make the capsules stick together, however. Once out of the freezer, they should be used quickly.

Capsules From Flowers

Capsules from marijuana flowers can be made in much the same way they are made with leaf. Just process the flowers into a flour (see page 13) and follow the directions above.

The biggest difference in using flowers is the dose. For safety it is prudent to use the smaller size capsules which hold about .2 grams. One or two of these capsules will give most people a good buzz. Doses of .5 grams or more is a strong dose of good sinsemilla flowers. See the dosage section (page 9) for more information.

Arthritis Capsules

Use flax or hemp oil as the oil for making the capsules. These oils have anti-inflammatory effects, as does the pot.

Topical Medicines

Marijuana can be made into salves or creams that can be applied for local pain relief from muscle aches, or inflamed joints. Folk remedies often prescribed poultices made of marijuana for medical conditions such as rheumatism. Salves can also be applied, like tiger balm, for headaches near the surface of the skin. Some people also use the salve for skin conditions such as psoriasis.

The best way to make these medicines is with a base of marijuana oil (see page 21). The oil can be applied directly to the skin. Or you can make a salve by mixing together on low heat, 5 parts of marijuana oil, and 1 part bee's wax. When thoroughly heated and mixed pour into a container and cool. You can substitute other medicinal oils for part of the marijuana oil.

What kind of oil to use in making the marijuana oil is your choice. Olive or corn oil are good oils to use if the marijuana oil is going to be used for both cook-ing and topical application. If you are only going to use the oil externally you can use coconut oil, or even cocoa butter. If you do use cocoa butter use the marijuana butter recipe on page 19. Massage oils can also be used.

Most people don't report getting high by topically applying marijuana. Still, someone not used to marijuana, or someone using a lot of it, may feel some slight effect. A full body massage with marijuana oil will definitely get you high, and could be excessive. Try only a back massage the first time, to gauge how you like the experience.

Government Issued Pot

Don't look to the government to supply you with "choice" marijuana anytime soon. The DEA does continue to provide marijuana from the government's pot farm in Mississippi, to a few sick people. The bad news is the marijuana being distributed is of poor quality for smoking. It consists of cut leaf rather than flower tops. Seems marijuana flowers jam up the government's rolling machine. If you were sold this pot you would probably feel you got burned.

The pot has a standardized 2% THC level and comes rolled in joints. Since so few people receive pot from the government it is not really necessary to critique its quality other to say this pot would better be used for cooking. Most people would smoke this pot only if they had nothing else.

A non-government
pot farm

illnesses treated with cannabis

Glaucoma

One of the first illnesses marijuana was legally made available for, though only two people currently get pot for treatment.

Marijuana has proven effective in reducing ocular pressure that damages the eye over time. Glaucoma is the second leading cause of blindness in the United States. At least half of the patients with glaucoma cannot tolerate the drugs prescribed for the illness. Many questions have been raised about the efficacy of the drugs available for treating glaucoma.

Thank the L.A. Police for finding out that pot lowered the pressure in the eye. Never mind that at the time they were trying to prove that pot dilated the eye's pupil, (it doesn't) and were going to use the finding as cause to arrest people.

It has been proven in animal studies that eye drops made with Cannabis will lower eye pressure. A compress made with marijuana tea is soothing to the eyes, but I have been unable to verify its medicinal properties. However, a pharmaceutical company in Jamaica has reportedly marketed such an eye drop product, called Cannasol. Though it is not available in the U.S. it is reportedly available on some islands in the Caribbean.

Asthma

Certain kinds of Cannabis are known to have expectorant qualities useful in the treatment of Asthma. It may not be THC which is the most useful cannabinoid in this condition. The terpenes, the aromatic, non-psychoactive volatile oils, which give marijuana flowers their distinctive smell, may also play a part.

More research is needed in this area.

Though most people who use marijuana for asthma smoke it, vaporization may be the best method of ingestion. Rather than burned, the flowers are heated until their oils are vaporized. This allows the person to inhale the useful gases at a lower temperature. A few smokeless pipes, which do this, are on the market.

Cancer

Marijuana is used to stimulate appetite during chemo and radiation therapy for cancer patients. Marijuana stimulates appetite, both when eaten and when smoked, although the medicinal effects last longer when the grass is eaten. Patients suffering from nausea may smoke a joint initially, then follow up by eating marijuana when they can hold down food.

Marijuana is also helpful for pain relief associated with cancer. Eating marijuana is more effective and long lasting for relieving pain, providing relief for up to 12 hours.

Marijuana has been adopted by cancer patients because it is more effective, with fewer side effects than many of the pharmaceutical drugs available. By now, it is the worst kept secret on many chemotherapy wards. The nausea from chemotherapy can be life threatening in itself, as many patients experience rapid declines in weight from an inability to keep food down .

Marinol is legal as an anti-nausea drug in the treatment of cancer. Patients using Marinol have given it mixed reports. Many people report that marijuana is more effective than Marinol. The strategy of one patient was to store Marinol in case his supply of marijuana ran out. This points out one of the real problems faced by sick people using marijuana— it is not always available. For recreational users, a drought might be just an annoyance, but to the very

Thank the L.A. Police for finding out that pot lowered the pressure in the eye.

For recreational
users, a drought
might be just an
annoyance, but to
the very sick it can
be life-threatening.

ill it can be more serious, even life-threatening.

Aids

Marijuana is used primarily to stimulate the appetite of people with this illness. It is also used for pain relief, and as a general reviver of spirit. Both smoked and eaten marijuana are helpful in treating the symptoms of AIDS.

Most AIDS patients who use marijuana for appetite stimulation or to ward off nausea, smoke marijuana, at least initially. When marijuana is eaten, however, these medical effects last much longer, sometimes up to 12 hours. Many patients use a combination of marijuana therapies, either smoking or eating the marijuana, depending on how they feel.

Marinol is approved in the treatment of AIDS. Patients report varying results from its use.

Migrane Headaches

Smoking marijuana has been found to be somewhat effective against migraine headaches, particularly those caused by stress. Oral ingestion is a better option for long term pain relief.

Multiple Sclerosis

MS is a auto-immune disorder in which the nerve sheaths throughout the body are attacked by a person's own immune system. MS is a chronic illness which, though it does go into remission, can get worse over time.

Many people with MS have reported good results smoking marijuana at the onset of an attack. Because marijuana gets into the body's system quickly when smoked, it is the preferred method of ingestion. It is also possible that eating marijuana could be helpful on "bad days" if they can be anticipated. The anti-inflammatory effect experienced when marijuana is eaten may also be helpful in the long term suppression of this condition.

Marinol may also be helpful, though it is presently not approved for this use.

Spasms

Marijuana is helpful in calming many kinds of spasms such as those related to spinal cord injuries and muscles spasms. Smoking, rather than eating, is preferred because relief comes quickly when taken in this manner. Eating marijuana is more effective for pain relief.

Menstrual Cramping

Small amounts of marijuana cooked into food or teas (see Teas) are helpful in treating cramps.

Epilepsy

One of the historic uses of Cannabis preparations were as anti-convulsant to control seizures of all kinds. Epilepsy is a chronic disease that, when active, is characterized by large or small seizures.

There is a strong movement of people with this illness who are medicating themselves with marijuana. This is because marijuana, in many cases, seems more effective than the medicines available with fewer side effects. Strong barbiturates and anti-convulsant drugs like Dilantin are frequently prescribed for epilepsy. Though smoking marijuana can be used to quickly get the drug into the body when needed, eating marijuana is helpful for long term relief.

Patients usually continue using prescribed medication with marijuana. Marijuana does work with anti-convulsant drugs.

Marinol could be effective against epilepsy but it has not been studied or approved.

Until 1937, Marijuana extract was legal in the U.S. and used to treat a number of ailments. Photo courtesy Tod Mikuriya, M.D. from *Marijuana: Medical Papers*

Anorexia

Marinol is approved for patients with this eating disorder though many doctors are reluctant to prescribe it, especially when cost is a consideration. Both smoking and eating marijuana are known to stimulate the appetite.

Arthritis and Inflammatory Conditions

When eaten, marijuana has both analgesic and anti-inflammatory effects. This can be helpful in both Osteo and Rheumatoid arthritis, when joints become swollen and painful. A common folk remedy for swollen joints is a poultice of marijuana leaves and oil wrapped around the inflamed area. Alcohol extracts (see page 16) can be used to make a poultice. Also see the topical medicine section on page 76.

A few patients getting Marinol for other illnesses report that it is somewhat effective, though unapproved, for arthritis.

Patients also report using marijuana as a bridge drug that helps them slowly wean themselves off addictive steroid drugs, like prednisone, which are often indiscriminately prescribed for arthritis.

Insomnia

Many people report help getting to sleep by using marijuana. Smoking is the preferred method of ingestion. The variety of Cannabis smoked seems also important. Indica varieties can be sleepy although almost any pot can lead some people to the dreamtime.

Other Conditions

Many other medical conditions have been treated with marijuana. Much anecdotal information is available showing that marijuana can be effective in treating alcohol and other drug (opiates, cocaine) addictions. As these three types of drugs are implicated in a high percentage of the crime committed in the United States, this matter needs to be studied. Marijuana leaf cigarettes have also been used as an aid in quitting tobacco smoking.

Since marijuana is primarily a recreational drug, one may not readily think of it as a medicine. The question of why is it used recreationally is important. Like other recreational drugs it is used to relieve tension. In today's hustle and bustle world tension can be a real problem, and it is implicated in many medical conditions. Millions of people have found release from stress and mild depression with marijuana.

Other reports show that some cannabinoids in marijuana have antibiotic qualities. This could turn out to be quite important as the effectiveness of available antibiotics wane.

The discovery of the receptor sites in the brain and spleen to which THC binds opens up a whole new area of medical research and possibility. The body produces its own chemical, anandamide, which also binds to these receptors. The word is derived from the Sanskrit, "ananda", meaning "bliss". Anandamide is found in areas of the brain that regulate memory, coordination of movement, and emotions. According to Jonathan Ott in *Pharmacotheon*, finding anandamide constitutes the discovery of a new class of neurotransmitters which the body uses for relaxation, and perhaps, for "bliss". The cannabis puzzle, how and why it works on the body and mind, is being explored.

The question remains— will the information be used to broaden medical and scientific research, or to put more people in jail?

index